THE MISSING MONTHS

by the same author

poetry
MONTEREY CYPRESS
THE COAST OF BOHEMIA
THE JUPITER COLLISIONS
SMALL HOURS
DOVES

non-fiction
ELIOT, AUDEN, LOWELL: ASPECTS OF
THE BAUDELAIREAN INHERITANCE
SHAKESPEARE THE AESTHETE:
AN EXPLORATION OF LITERARY THEORY
THE LIVES OF ELSA TRIOLET

LACHLAN MACKINNON

The Missing Months

faber

First published in 2022
by Faber & Faber Ltd
Bloomsbury House
74–77 Great Russell Street
London WC1B 3DA

Typeset by Hamish Ironside
Printed in the UK by TJ Books Ltd, Padstow, Cornwall

A CIP record for this book is available from the British Library

ISBN 978–0–571–37538–7

FSC
www.fsc.org
MIX
Paper from
responsible sources
FSC® C013056

2 4 6 8 10 9 7 5 3 1

To Ruth Morse and Stefan Collini

Acknowledgements

Some of these poems have previously appeared in *Ambit* and *The Spectator*.

Poets used not to acknowledge their editors. Now we do. I am happy to thank, at Faber, Matthew Hollis for his acute, astute eye, Jane Feaver, Lavinia Singer and Rali Chorbadzhiyska for their help and support, and Hamish Ironside for his perspicacity.

I want to thank Alan Jenkins, who once edited a book-length manuscript of mine overnight without being asked. He has not seen these poems but has over many years and many shrewd readings become an editorial conscience for me and, I suspect, many poets of my generation and younger.

Wendy Cope and Jane Feaver combined forces to convince me one poem needed clarification.

Malcolm Hebron discovered the Judge Jeffreys story.

Contents

I

II

III

The Missing Months

IV

I

A Pang

i.m. Patrick Lowman

1940–2009

I'm sure you knew
but left it –

that I was shamefully completely
wrong about Jaan Kaplinski.

Postman shopkeeper
bits and bobs when I knew you,

your father beat you literate.
You skipped school,
worked on the barrows,
went for a soldier.

Men from your regiment
looked you up,
wry reliable friend.

Some came the day your wicker
basket was put
cold under soil among trees,
stars and the wind.

You're always no longer
there when I go back –

a face on the pub wall
with wiry grey
swept hair.

About Kaplinski, Pat –

forgive me.

Entropy

The stars will go.

They may clench or explode
but they will dissipate
into one flat field
of dwindling energies too weak
to reach for one another:
nothing at all will take shape.

Man will go long before.

A hundred thousand years,
a blink of weeds
rupturing concrete winds
levelling uprights
bricks crumbling back to sand
and there will be no trace.

My name will vanish.

Odd I can think about the weather
the day after my funeral.
I'd like a thin slant rain
needling the roots of grass, working
in earth. I'd like it
to be in spring, before the roses.

Dreams

I also
appear in dreams.

Happy or sad or hooting
over some dreadful pun

or puzzled, concentrated, silent.
I may be anything

I've never been, pilot or astronaut
or football player. What I say

may be truer than I can say,
hieratic, oracular.

Styx

i.m. Matthew Sweeney

1952–2018

As if seen
suddenly you
here
this long moment
in one eye
the fleck of blood
that worried me
that always worried me

Strange Gods

A place for persons to be purged
of personhood
to become viruses of light

where they forget
rank earth
breath of the first mow

where letter is law
dead hand and mortgage
paid heart and soul

song unison with no
wandering descant
dance measured

to such comely
uncomfortable eternity the poet
willing himself died

alive

Ryoanji

i.m. Geoff Hewitson, colleague, Second Master of Winchester College, former player and Chairman, Corinthian Casuals, friend, who came with me

1935–2018

I moved and grey stones moved
to prove it: stand wherever
and one stone disappears.
Raked gravel sea. Fleet under orders.

The garden is a whole
you can't hold. As it is
inside us. Outside. Always one
stone somewhere you do not see.

Here any stone may go
missing. Changeless
raked gravel tray. Here seeing
and being seen are always one thing.

After

Something had opened
and something had been released.

The moon shone on.
The skylight rain had ceased.

I had to sleep.
Sleep is a feast-day priest.

Poetry

Like being inside a paperweight
where shaken snow
rises:

Kremlin White House Father Christmas
or a bewildered penguin

whatever takes the storm
must stand up straight in it
and wait until it settles

itself again.

Thank You

I hand myself up the bus to the driver's end
to thank him. I climb off thanking him
because it's what we do thank
bus drivers as we thank
no one else it's a cultural thing
making ready perhaps
when the ferryman dumps us
on the sulphurous shore
to thank him too.

II

Snow-voice

after Paul Celan

To the end snow-voice, tree-high,
in tall wind fronting
forever
unwindowed huts:

planed dreams
shriek
and abrade corrugated ice;

shadows thrown from words
to hack free to stack
in rings round stooked wood
down ditches.

North European

Novels with characters
who don't have roomy
nineteenth-century selves.   ·

Novels for people who don't have
roomy
nineteenth-century lives.

Novels for people who are stretched thin.
A clean modern apartment
glass metal minimalist.

Solitudes.
Bewildering passions
today, long ago.

For preference bicycles.
Underfoot in the ice months
ice crinkles.

Ameonna

Rain walks with her she is always inside it
like a phone box with water windows or a hazy column
of slim separate lines or a buzzing cloud
like static

a bad guest for weddings
or funerals she brings damp
among the sandwiches the cooling tea

her bed is disappointment
you want to reach out lift the cloak away

like a cloche but there's nothing growing there

Cassandra

We too have secret police too
stupid to recognise themselves.

We have safe lifestyle poems.
We celebrate our gardens

sun-loungers food
and in our poems

the wind the longer shadows
foreshadow private sorrows.

Now the wind that is blowing blows
out of the future into now.

Vastation. Tumult.
Great population shifts.

Great vowel shifts
erasing nuance

distinction tense.
Ruinous purging years.

Summer of '17

I write from before.
You live in after.
I don't know what it's like there.

Here they hold
guilt is hereditary.
Those who vote wrong

are shouted down.
Like flagellants like men of Salem like
Red Guards they flock

and only settle to destroy
monuments figures legends
inscriptions Roman numbers.

One by one points of reference
are blanked. Among the ruins
I hope you find this letter.

From the *Hampshire Chronicle*

An eighteenth-century murder trial,
heard perhaps in the same Great Hall

as (I think it was there) Judge Jeffreys
had whispered silkily Give me names,

I love names.
I hope he got none.

The woman's name escapes me,
not the thought of her heart

hardened against herself
or the muttering creaturely

compassion of the people watching,
men, women, this example.

Beyond all doubt she had killed her baby,
beyond all doubt her guilty

singleness had, before that, driven her
stark mad.

In front of an aghast crowd
she pleaded guilty. Even the judge

was in tears, begging
she change her plea. She refused

so she had to be let go hang.

Fait divers

I see they've kept a pig's brain
alive almost an hour
after they delicately disconnected it

and raised it from the skull's urn
oxygenated, whole.
It is believed awareness

did not persist, though some low
level of consciousness
may have been possible.

Putative benefits cannot make me feel
the triumph of this
first-time feat.

No,
at some persistent low
level of consciousness my hands grind, terrified.

Kulturpessimismus

Institutions: ignore,
The press: ignore,
The yellow press
If there be better.

There is no better.
Go down all instruments
And brave band
Flash, oompah, trim.

College Street

I'm sitting in the outer office, waiting
for my appointment, and I'm gazing
at a street I've known, for some years
lived in, a quarter of a century.

Sun shines. A slightly hazy day
in early autumn. Suddenly within me
wet light and wet leaves whirl
in wind along the street

my marriage failed in. They
pointlessly make the sound
the years did not make, drifting in my hair.
I'm a middle-aged man. I rise to greet my boss.

Scholar

Easily led
from book to book
by a glint from the half-open
door of a footnote

sometimes
into dirty small choking
rooms I must run from
before my spirit dies

and sometimes into larger
airier spaces
with well-placed windows giving
on wide strange vistas.

It's a lifetime
from the four-year-old boy reporting
that morning's stories in *The Times*
to an elderly neighbour

who would stand by the fence
to listen to him,
breaking off whatever it is
men find to do in gardens.

Years later Voltaire would suggest I
cultivate mine.
I knew better
than take him literally.

He meant dig
into whatever small patch
you find fertile.
I tried

but watching sun slide
across the faceless
institutional wooden tables
the come-and-go

of the believing young,
the responsibly checked
impatience of their elders,
I have to wonder

was I right to refuse
the know-nothing travel
so many my age made
through places wars have ruined

paddy-field wisdom
a world of cheap red
dream-catching songlines
abasement and their harvest?

Not to have risked
absolute loss
is loss. Time passes
and we must leave the reading-room.

III

The Missing Months

Lockdown: Granddaughter

for Eira

Before

She is four she can say
Virus and lockdown

Laid down in her like a layer of soil
Black with the sacking of a city

Of a world she will not remember

Lockdown: Tim Pride, 1965–2020

Among the thirty thousand so far dead
The numbers who can never all be counted
This kind man

Alone at home

Spare funeral on line

The nine permitted mourners
The priest who knew him

The body to the fire
The soul to God who knows

Each one by name

Lockdown: A Walk

The rain drums its fingers and moves on

Sun comes
A dog barks

A bird squeaks like a hinge

With picnic-tables and lager
Narrowboats open up

Their people wave like friends

Pale green fresh leaves
Shake water from their hair

Lockdown: A Flight

We cannot sweep air clean
We can hope for a vaccine

At the boathouse a heron
Stalks the length of the concrete ramp

Disdainful stabs
Find nothing

So it heaves itself up
With its shoulders

Flight is a weighty matter
Requires serious thought

Don't interrupt
Until across the river

Above the trees
It stretches

Banks on a slope of air and turns

Free at last free at last

Lockdown: Sorting the Garage

Fishing about
I come on Mandelstam

Who has insomnia he has read half
The catalogue of ships in Homer

He wants to set sail
As love exacts

After all what was Troy without Helen
Men of Achaea

Some dusty burg

From any now the line to Homer
Is always open

Lockdown: Gloves

They're here again
The little boy with new red goalkeeping gloves
His older sister her blue-and-white dress

Yesterday
I kicked their ball back
Predictably wide

Today
They don't notice us
He is inside the bandstand
Its columns offer six goals
He saves and saves

Their schools are closed
But they have not stopped growing
We grow in watching

To them
To everybody
Through and beyond
This world a further calls

Lockdown: Brief Summer Release 1

for W.

False early summer
Bare sun
No traffic fumes to snag at breath or haze
High indifference of a brighter blue

A lilac close to this warm public bench
Infuses us with its familiar smell
Made strange by coming clean coming true

Lockdown: Dreaming Utopia

A city to hear your own footsteps in

Cafe terraces where people read poetry
They smile they drift they hover
They wander through museums galleries
All their explainers dumb with wonder

You stretch your hands out sideways
To catch the sun like bright fresh leaves

There
I shall speak to you from among the dead

Lockdown: If We Should Die

Still
Will be gone will return

Seasonal creatures
Balletic swifts

Games-masters running backwards blowing whistles
At their indifferent broken crocodiles of runners

Lockdown: The Capital

Dissolving city
Where the people no longer go

Or the high-rolling gangsters
Slave-owning princes
Attendant bankers

The Babel towers
Where cleaners earned more pride
In their work than the cleaned-for

(Who never met them)

City churning its young like
Shingle in surf

City of glimpses

A crawling bus a green
Man turning red

Impatience
Ground elder to the soul

Lockdown: The Provinces

Knowing everything
Gets its turn in the heat
The shyest flowers
Lie doggo thick
Leaves sheltering what soil they can

Pindar came out of Thebes that
Primitive place

Lockdown: Brief Summer Release 2

Here's evening
Housekeeping for tomorrow

Children pedalling homeward
As I imagine dust
Very slowly
Thickening in the boathouse

Lockdown: Our Bench Again

Death floats about us
Where we sit in history

It likes glass it likes handles
It fears copper it loves ice

It shows very little interest in food

It breaks up in sunlight
Soap disconnects it

At any moment any
One of us might be disconnected

Sent to the sci-fi world
Of masks machines

The hopeful drugged sleep
Many do not survive

Lockdown: Summer Fatigues

Dormer shadows
Black chimney shadows

Grass
Goes patchy camouflage
Crawls across earth on boring exercise

Air itches

Lockdown: Before Speech

The play area locked
We watch toddlers
Bumble about their business
Making their own fun

They run stiffly
That one her father picks up
Turns round and plonks down turns round
Stiffly runs past her mother's spread arms

Triangulates her parents runs between them

They move off
She resists following
Until a dam within her gives

She passes them
Pauses
A touch stooped
To scan intently
A patch of dry grass

Who
Dare pretend there is no
Free will

Lockdown: Thinking of Avigdor Arikha, 1929–2010

It's lonely watching how the rain runs down
It's warming watching how the rain runs down

The afternoons revive with television
The afternoons expire with television

A man obsessed with seeing what he saw
Brought out the age-old glass Venetian bowl

He'd almost made a spectre of itself
By painting it so close to evanescence

A thing of light amid a world of light.
He held it up for me to see the light

Which was the day's light over mansard roofs
In Paris near the jail called Santé (Health)

Lockdown: Starless

Nights are tangled
Past wrongs
By others by myself

Visions of herded
Conscripted labour

No smartphone functioning
No phone
No landline even

No messages

To   From

Nobody
Nobody answers
Anything

Lockdown: Jan 2021

She'll be too old
For the climbing frame next year

Red jacket
Pointy hat

Trees gilded
By mid-afternoon

Good luck child
Good luck

Lockdown: Keeper of the Flame

On YouTube Miranda Lambert
Sings to and for
Past country singers

The torch she carries
Country music
Is three chords and the truth

She stops and steps clear
Flings back an arm
Yells Give it up

For my amazing band

IV

Between Cities

Long after sunset
they are borne in a box of light.

Some peer out, some talk,
inspect phones, dream or read.

One or two sleep
as they ride over darkness.

For most, world is reduced,
ribbon

like a typewriter ribbon,
bumpy, irregularly marked, grass

and concrete, traces
of the invisible

beyond, trusted to be there
still, as it was.

Herefordshire, 2019

for Fiona and Peter

Ah Karen this
is twice as steep and not your stepped
Yorkshire garden it minds me of
we played in
more than half a century back not

here where my grown-up writer friends
ted hay in a fenced stall
nextdoor their bantams
uttering thick
rich eggs.

Inside, a dog vets me
from the conservatory
through an inner window.
Below it, things are laid out
like a pocket Morandi –

small stoppered glazed green jar
and smaller desert-coloured
matt-and-gloss pouting jug.
On a high shelf
the balanced off-centre

arc of a rank of jars
shows eye and order
two studies differently observe
in this house tight
against its hill.

I'm sitting like a grown-up
looking and sounding like a grown-up
to the sudden happy
amazement of a boy
whose best friend is a girl

near Leeds in 1962.

Kite

A brown paper kite
lifts and stoops
on a moor above Leeds
flutters and plummets
never quite taking full

strength from the wind
that urges it
tugging my hand
my child hand
and my father is not there

who made it
and might imagine it
pulling for freedom
the way I one day must.

True Happy Stories

My father played for Harlequins once.

In summer the great rugger players
put out a cricket team and, their slow bowler stuck
on a delayed train, my father was deputed
from the home, the schoolmasters', side.

Their whites gleam
with Corinthian spirit
long, long ago.

Dr Grace, waking early, fished his hosts'
ornamental fountain
of all its goldfish.

Things happen as they should
long, long ago
in the endless imagined summers
that never were,

until they'd vanished, deathless.

A Young Woman in 1989

Having walked her outside
I suddenly found I'd
hugged her tight as she cried.
She had just certified

my father's death, and I
held and let her cry,
sensing why.
He was her first to die.

It hurt her, though as she'd said
upping the morphine led
to sleep. No coughing blood.
I almost kissed her head.

Gossip

for Caroline

Rain whips
Karl Marx and you
as when we buried you
that muddy day.

What can I tell you?
Everyone's well but Simon
who also died young. The sisterhood is scattered
Anna in Czechia

others abroad
and some in London.
You wouldn't recognise me
my grey hair.

Your world is fading
like a radio signal
when the rain gets heavy –

hurtling out past the furthest planet.

Drawings by Henri Michaux

I see a kukri
a body lying
a dancer flinging arms

a baby tumbling
nappy bulging a man clinging
like drowning to a quarterstaff

a camel on its back
under a cross
a couple kissing

a thing with two legs
neck blown like smoke long
tyrannosaurus head

splotches and moons
and nothing drawn
attention to

flat time
appalling flat time
stuck time

there are wells of time
frozen over
in ill years

I couldn't bear
music or read
through any page

I see my own
face looking back
uncombed wax-white

Cufflinks

i.m. D.

1956–2017

Dreck and bling. Joe Allen. Seventies yet.
Butt-ends and younger sisters
of half-remembered titles.
Your gossip. Monica Lewinsky's
first London trip. The living Habsburgs.

For nigh on forty years
begasped eye-raising star
through all becoming
my oldest friend
until your mother died

and you went mad
Nazi leather mad
vortex of boys mad
cocaine mad.
Slow-release

in suppository form, it hit once
while you were chatting with the Prince of Wales.
I heard it saw it what it did
a later evening.
Toward the end

we had your scowl
airbrushed out of our wedding photographs.
Junior ministers musicians peers
activists writers academics
socialites networked at your cremation

but no one from the last
self-loathing months.
Establishment eulogy
cars and a pub you might have used.
They found your body days dead.

Trusted in many worlds (no diary)
the world closed over you.

.   .   .   .

I'd bought black cufflinks
flat chips of stone

for funerals.
Once we'd have giggled but
so yes my dear I wore them.
Years ago years and with a Lords'
Clerkship to risk

you kept on visiting
a friend in prison, quite properly in prison.
We called when she was free.
She had a rentboy with her. Not for her.
More than four decades ring

with laughter like a high
hall, Christ Church Hall.
I'll never phone again and get that
wrong number and the patient Spanish woman –
over and over through the decades.

I hope she's older than us both
and as you would that she is vigorously some
scarred monstrous glittering triumphant age.

Smoke

i.m. Joe Bain, colleague, friend

1928–2011

Nursery food, gin, a magazine of cigarettes –

Now your man Hughes, you see, looks like a Laureate.
Tennyson. Mad as a hatter, naturally. Your man Scott. Gide.
Polyolbion: some surprisingly good bits.

The long-drawn late-night phone calls after you retired,
the last few passages to trace for *Nemo's Almanac*.
Once, I did recognise a bench in *Adam Bede*.

A late night at the piano, one by one
ghosts of nineteenth-century composers, names
we summoned from your shadows, wandered in,

making you vary harmony and tempo
before you demonstrated
all rock'n'roll comes from the Bay State hymnals.

When the neighbours' grape hyacinths push
their heads out through the stems of tiny hedges
I see white faces rise from rear stage,

prisoners made free men, your production of *Fidelio*.
You looked like Edward VII in his heyday.
You couldn't teach, you said, without some background noise.

To live without God as though God existed.
Without Beethoven I might not have stood it.
Blank loneliness. Laughed a lot, smoked a lot, your man Bain.

Praise-Song for Les Murray, 1938–2019

When your folk were trapped in wooden walls
four-square where you were born raw poor
your grown eyes bulged near burst and you broke

head down straight through the barn door
to open air and hauled breath
to say names for new things you saw.

When bad old things took new forms the truth
you spoke then was not liked. As if you'd care.
It cost you and you kept your path.

Good things you saw you showed with shaped air.
Verse is not meant to praise in our time.
It is meant to despair. Praise is a kind of prayer.